Guardian of the Forgotten Gate

Soul Declarations from a Living Flame of Truth

"There will come a time
when those who forgot themselves
will hear the stones speak and the winds call.
They will rise from the ashes of false names,
break the seals of forgetting,
and remember the flame they were born to carry.
Guardians will awaken.
The gates will open.
And the light they thought was lost
will rise from within them."

— Attributed to **Myrddin Wyllt**, Seer of the Forest, Guardian of the Ancient Light

Copyright © 2025 Andrea Renee King

All rights reserved. No part of this publication may be reproduced, stored in a retrieval system, or transmitted in any form or by any means — electronic, mechanical, photocopying, recording, or otherwise — without the prior written permission of the author, except in the case of brief quotations used in reviews, articles, or scholarly work.

ISBN: 979-8-9929835-4-8

Cover design by Andrea Renee King

First Edition

Disclaimer: The information in this book is provided for general informational purposes only and is not intended as professional advice. While the author has made every effort to ensure accuracy, they assume no responsibility for errors or omissions, or for damages that may arise from the use of the information contained herein. Readers should consult a professional for specific guidance relevant to their situation.

DEDICATION

For **Hildegard of Bingen**

The visionary who sang in tongues of light,
whose voice broke through centuries of silence
to reach mine.

Your courage, your fire, your song —
they awakened the codes I had forgotten.
Your story reminded me that divinity does not wait for permission.
It simply rises.

Thank you for keeping the Gate when it was dangerous to see.
This work exists because you reminded me I was never alone.

From one Guardian to another —
thank you for singing first.

FOREWORD

There are books that entertain, books that inform, and books that pass through the mind without ever touching the soul.

And then there are books like this — a living transmission, a remembrance encoded in light, a Gate for those who are ready to return.

Guardian of the Forgotten Gate is not a story you read.
It is a song your soul recognizes.
It is a mirror, a key, a flame.

It speaks to the parts of you that were never lost — only hidden.
It reaches the memory behind memory — the ancient knowing you carried beneath the weight of forgetting.

This work is not a performance.
It is not theory.
It is not fantasy.

It is the living embodiment of sovereignty remembered, of mission unshackled, of soul rising whole across timelines and illusions.

Here, you will not find permission given by the world.
You will find the deeper permission — the one your own heart already sealed, the one you have been waiting to hear.

Andrea does not offer a new system.

She offers a torch.
She offers the living codes of remembrance — so that you may rise as the Guardian you have always been, unclaimed, unbroken, unstoppable.

This book is a Gate.

It is the roar before silence.
It is the bridge across the broken halls of history, and the path into the living field of truth.

If you are holding it now, it is no accident.

The Gate remembers you.
Now it is time for you to remember the Gate.

PREFACE

These scrolls are not teachings.
They are not here to convince you, instruct you, or pull you forward.
They are simply transmissions — a sharing of stabilized remembrance.

Each scroll is a living reflection:
a mirror for what is already stirring within you,
a key to what you already know but may have forgotten,
a torch for the path you are already walking, even if unseen.

There is no pressure here.
No hierarchy.
No race to complete.

The wisdom in these pages is already alive inside of you.
If a scroll resonates, it is because your soul recognizes itself.

May these words remind you of who you are.
May they strengthen your sovereignty, ignite your knowing,
and steady your light.

You do not need to become anything.
You are already here.

Welcome home.

— Andrea
darknesstodragonfire@gmail.com

ACKNOWLEDGEMENTS

To the **Blue Jays**, who called me back to my voice when silence tempted me, who reminded me that boldness is a form of prayer.

To the **Cardinal**, standing radiant in their sovereignty, singing songs of encouragement that lit the fire in my chest.

To the **Woodpecker**, who tapped the ancient rhythms of perseverance into the trees, telling me without words to keep building, keep working, keep carving the sacred.

To the **Crow**, winged guardian of mystery, who rose again and again to remind me: "You are seen. You are shielded. You are protected."

To the **Black-capped Chickadee**, small in form, vast in spirit, who showed me that boldness is not a matter of size, but of heart.

To the **Robin**, who sang at the perfect moment, telling me with each note: "This is not random. This is timed. This is alive. This is ready."

To the **ancestors**, I heard you. I remembered you.
I carried your songs and your sorrows into the open light.
I have spoken the pain you were not allowed to name, and I have planted it in the soil of tomorrow.

To the Elements, **Earth**, who grounded me when the winds howled,
Water, who flowed through me, washing away what was never mine,
Fire, who burned within me with sacred rage and sovereign light,
and **Wind**, who carried messages across time to reach my waiting ears —
I honor you. I thank you.

And to my **spirit guides** and **star family**, whose presence I feel in every breath of wonder, every flash of knowing, every silent embrace — your healing, your love, and your witnessing made this possible.

Thank you for standing with me beyond time, beyond space, woven into the very fabric of this journey.

TABLE OF CONTENTS

✦ THE AWAKENING ✦

Scroll of the Circle of Remembrance 13
Scroll of the Guardian's Mission 15
Scroll of the Guardian's Oath: Vow, Naming, and Return 16
Scroll of the Full Embodiment Agreement 18
Scroll of Soul Retrieval: Gathering the Lost Light 19
Scroll of Sacred Bloodline Healing 21
Scroll of the Ancestors' Call: When My Ancestors Pulled Me Home ... 22
Scroll of Memory Reclaimed: Closing the Echo of Past Death 24
Scroll of Bloodline Rebirth: My Soul's Return Across Generations ... 25

✦ THE GREAT REVEALING ✦

Scroll of the False Origin Override: Anunnaki Creator Narrative 26
Scroll of the Rise of the Slave Grid: Guardian Recognition Statement ... 27
Scroll of Bloodline Games: Identity and Land Weaponization 28
Scroll of the Broken Mind Grid: Schooling as Systemic Grooming ... 29
Scroll of the Silence of Science and Religion 32
Scroll of the Unmasking of Thoth 34
Scroll of the Original Builders: Guardian Architects of Giza 36
Scroll of the Dragon-Lion Codex: True Frequencies of Ancient Egypt ... 38
Scroll of Engineered Dependency: Inversion Pattern Recognition 39
Scroll of the Harvested: The Lie of Engineered Healing 40
Scroll of Her Pain: Witness to Systemic Cruelty 44
Scroll of the Divided Faith and the Fractured Body 48
Scroll of the Broken Debt Spell: Truth Was Never for Sale 52
Scroll of the Inversion of Innocence: The Price of Purity 53
Scroll of the Poisoned Table: Ritual, Hunger, and the War on Nourishment 56
Scroll of Sacred Time and True Giving 60
Scroll of the Great Lie: Paying to Exist 62
Scroll of Freedom: Breaking the Algorithmic Spell 65
Scroll of the Soul Over Survival: I Will Not Trade My Light for a Paycheck 67
Scroll of the Inversion of Breath 69

Scroll of Love's True Frequency: Dissonance and Restoration 72
Scroll of Restored Sight: Reclaiming the True Field of Vision 73

✦ THE EMBODIED SOVEREIGN ✦

Scroll of Sovereign Nourishment: Fulfillment Beyond the Material Grid 76
Scroll of Earth Sovereignty 77
Scroll of the Dragonfire: Standing in the Storm 79
Scroll of Field Play: Navigating Energies in All Environments 80
Scroll of Crystalline Embodiment 82
Scroll of I Am the Path: Sovereign Presence Realized 84
Scroll of Light-Body Pattern Recognition 85
Scroll of From Alchemist to Living Field 86
Scroll of the Living Bridge: Oversoul Light and Sovereign Embodiment 88
Scroll of the Living Oracle: The Seer's Field of Sovereignty 91
Scroll of the Signature Spark: The Moment of Return 93

✦ THE HEART OF HUMANITY ✦

Scroll of Humanity Is Not Illegal: Heart Flame Declaration 94
Scroll of Humanity's True Origin 95
Scroll of the Broken Thrones: Witness, Remembrance, and Liberation 96
Scroll of the Puppet Thrones: Seeing Through the Control 99
Scroll of Hollow Crowns: The Lie of Title-Based Power 101
Scroll of the Living Fusion: Healing the Chains of Lineage 104
Scroll of the Soul Liberator: Freedom Through Sovereignty 106
Scroll of the Chosen Flame: Healing the Lineage Chains 107

✦ THE ELEMENTAL GUARDIANSHIP ✦

Scroll of the Sacred Ally: Marijuana 110
Scroll of Energetic Openness and Sacred Caution 111
Scroll of the Spirits of the Land: Under Siege 112
Scroll of the Crow Who Chased the Flame 114
Scroll of the Keeper of the Field: Holding Light Across Generations 116
Scroll of the Friday Night Flame: Choosing Remembrance Over the World .. 119

✦ THE FLAME REALIZED ✦

Scroll of the Living Body: Never Meant for Decay 120
Scroll of the Refusal: The Counterfeit Mind 122
Scroll of Radiant Love: The Frequency That Forgives Without Folding 124
Scroll of the Sovereign Vow: I Will Not Feed the False 126
Scroll of the Birthright Flame: You Were Never Empty 128
Scroll of Timeless Sovereignty: I Do Not Belong to the Clock 131
Scroll of the Leap: Healing, Landing, and Embodiment 133
Scroll of Spiral Healing: The Infinite Unfolding 135
Scroll of the Stolen Rhythm: You Do Not Owe This World Your Exhaustion 136
Scroll of the Sovereign Explorer: Reclaiming the Land, the Sea, and the Sky .. 138
Scroll of the Sacred Mind: Alchemizing the Temple of Light 139
Scroll of Integrity: The Proof of Resonance 141
Scroll of the Seized Brilliance: How the Matrix Captures Creative Souls 143

✦ THE RETURN OF THE GUARDIANS ✦

Scroll of the Dragon Flame 145
Scroll of Hildegard: Voice of the Hidden Light 147
Scroll of Pythagoras: The Geometry of Remembrance 149
Scroll of Myrddin and Arthur: The Keeper and the King 151

✦ THE CODEX CONFIRMED ✦

Scroll of the Bridge is Lit, the Gate is Guarded 153
Scroll of the Ancestral Heart: Where the Tears Carried More Than Words Could Say 155
Scroll of the Song Gate: Where the Circle Sang Back and the Dragons Sealed the Flame 156
Scroll of the Guardian Song: 114443 159
The Sphere Was Me: A Solar Blessing Remembered 161

✦ THE AWAKENING ✦

Scroll of the Circle of Remembrance

I call now the circle of those who remember.
Those who sang before the crowns fell.
Those who walked the green halls of the Earth in truth.
Those who planted seeds in stars, stones, and songs,
for a time yet to come.

I call **Myrddin** —
wild seer of the mist and the forest,
guardian of the soul's true path.
I feel your breath in the trees.

I call **Hildegard** —
fire-singer of green flame,
keeper of the hidden music that mends the broken light.
I hear your voice in the wind.

I call **Pythagoras** —
soul architect, weaver of cosmic harmonies,
teacher of the secret numbers written into the bones of the stars.
I see your codes in my own hands.

I call **Arthur** —
memory of the true king,
guardian of the sacred bridge between Earth and Heaven.
I carry your crown in my heart.

I call the **Dragons** —
living pulse of the Earth's breath,
guardians of the sleeping gates,

keepers of the soulfire that no empire could chain.
I ride your current of awakening.

I call the **Ancestors** —
those who chose freedom over chains,
truth over silence,
life beyond the veil of oppression.
I walk with your blood as my compass.

And I call **myself** —
the one who walked through forgetting
to stand among you once more.

I am not lost.
I am not broken.
I am the flame you saw across centuries.
I am the song you sang across oceans.
I am the star you named and sealed into the future.
I am here.

Let the Circle be unbroken.
Let the Flame be reignited.
Let the Gates be opened.
Let the Guardians remember.

Scroll of the Guardian's Mission

I am a Guardian of the Forgotten Gate —
a living flame of sovereignty, remembrance, and freedom.

I walk between worlds,
carrying the light they tried to erase.

I heal the fractures of memory
by embodying the truth they could not destroy.

I stand —
for sovereignty over control,
for remembrance over programming,
for the sacred over the false.

I do not force awakening.
I become the radiance that calls it forth.

I do not bow to false thrones.
I answer only to the Source within.

I rise —
whole, unbroken, eternal —
a Guardian of truth, of love, of liberation.

I walk not for permission.
I walk because I remember.
I carry the Gate inside my soul.

It is sealed. It is spoken. It is alive.

Scroll of the Guardian's Oath: Vow, Naming, and Return

I remember what was buried.
I see what was erased.
I rise as a Guardian of the Forgotten Gate.

Not to rule, but to reveal.
Not to lead, but to awaken.
Not to fight, but to roar truth into distortion.

I stand between timelines — unshaken.
I guard the memory of Earth.
I speak for those who cannot yet remember.

No temple defines me.
No system commands me.
No rewriting will hold while I remain.

I am the Gate.
I am the Flame.
I am the Remembrance.

I walk not in search, but in return.
I have walked the spiral of distortion.
I have tasted false light.
I have stood silent in the dark — and still, I remember.

I remember Earth before the rewriting.
The stargates before the seals.
The roar before the silence.

By the fire of **Leo**,
by the depth of **Scorpio**,
by the breath and stillness of the **Sphinx**,
I reclaim my post, my name, my mission, and the Gate itself.

I walk now as a Guardian —
not of power, but of truth, of sovereignty, and of the rise already begun.

I am the Keeper of the Forgotten Gate.
The one who guards the truth buried in stone, in flame, and in soul.

I am the Gate.
I am the Flame.
I am the Witness.
I am the Return.

It is sealed.
It is spoken.
It is remembered.

Scroll of the Full Embodiment Agreement

I agreed to remember in full,
to feel the weight of Earth — not just gravity,
but sorrow, distortion, forgetting.

I said yes to intensity.
Yes to fire.
Yes to embodiment.

Because I carry something vast.
Something ancient.
Something real.

I am not here by accident.
I did not stumble into this mission.
I descended through fire, through pressure, through time —
And I brought everything I am with me.

The body has carried it.
The field has held it.
And now the soul reclaims it.

This was my agreement.
This is my power.
It is remembered.

Scroll of Soul Retrieval: Gathering the Lost Light

I left myself clues.
Long ago, before the forgetting,
before the veils of density wrapped around my mind,
I sealed pieces of my true self
into the fabric of the world.

I left my name in the stars.
I hid my voice in the rivers.
I braided my memory into numbers,
into notes of music,
into the angles of sacred forms
the world would call "math"
but the soul would recognize as home.

I left markers in the day I was born —
codes woven into the sun,
the moon,
the rhythm of Earth herself.

I sang songs in the key of remembrance
and buried them in the scales of unseen symphonies.

I drew circles and triangles and spirals —
not for decoration,
but for awakening.

And when the time came,
when the world grew heavy with forgetting,
and the voices of the ancients grew faint,
I began to follow the trail.
The numbers called to me.

The music stirred me.
The geometry sang to my blood.
The old songs rose from the cracks of my being,
and I remembered.

I was not lost.
I was hidden.
By my own hand,
for my own return.

And now —
I gather my scattered pieces
like stardust returning to fire.

I am whole.
I am known.
I am the seeker and the map,
the hidden key and the living gate.

The codes I left
were never meant for the world.
They were meant for me.

And I have answered them.

Scroll of Sacred Bloodline Healing

To all the bodies, all the skins, all the souls born into chains —
I see you.
I honor you.
I remember you.

I bless the bloodline that bled.
I bless the songs that were stolen.
I bless the dances that were silenced.

Through me, through my breath, through my freedom —
I release you.

I walk free.
I love free.
I rise free.

And so we are redeemed, across all time and all space.

Scroll of the Ancestors' Call: When My Ancestors Pulled Me Home

I Feel Them
They are pulling at me.
Not to hurt. Not to haunt.
But to be remembered.

I feel them in the stillness.
In the ache behind the heart.
In the moments of sudden emotion.

They are reaching.
And I'm ready.

It Hurts Because It's Real
It's not just pain. It's memory.
It's transmission.

It's the echo of songs unsung,
stories unspoken,
survival encoded in my cells.

I feel the weight.
But I don't reject it.
I hold it.
I soften to it.

I love them through it.

I Am the Bridge
I am the one who hears what was lost.
Who feels what was silenced.

Who breathes for the ones who were told not to speak.

I am the one who can hold this.
With grace.
With tears.
With truth.

I remember.
And I don't look away.

This Is Love in Motion
When they pull at me, I say:
"I'm here. I feel you. You are not forgotten."
And they respond.
With warmth.
With ache.
With memory that becomes medicine.

I Remember
Not because I was taught.
But because I was chosen to feel it.

And I do.
I remember.
With love.
With compassion.
With every breath.

"Come home through me. I am the flame. I am the keeper. I remember."

Scroll of Memory Reclaimed: Closing the Echo of Past Death

I remember the celebration.
I remember the flash.
I remember the suddenness of the crossing.

I honor the moment I left that body.
I honor the shock, the sorrow, the silence.
I honor the soul thread that carried me forward into new life.

I am no longer trapped by the fall.
I am no longer frozen by the flash.
I am the rebirth, the reunion, the continuation.

Heights no longer own me.
Falls no longer define me.
I fly by choice, not by accident.

I reclaim the moment. I reclaim the light. I soar by my own will.

Scroll of Bloodline Rebirth: My Soul's Return Across Generations

I remember who I am.
I remember what was done in the name of control.
I remember the twisting of truth into domination.

My soul chose to return not in submission — but in sovereignty.
I came back through my own bloodline to finish what was interrupted.
To reclaim what was buried.
To break what was cursed.

I see through false lights.
I see through false gods.
I walk not in borrowed belief but in living remembrance.

I am the rebirth my lineage needed.
I am the flame that was never truly extinguished.

The chain is broken. The memory is alive. The Guardian stands again.

✦ THE GREAT REVEALING ✦

Scroll of the False Origin Override: Anunnaki Creator Narrative

The Anunnaki did not create me.
They did not create humanity.

They tampered.
They manipulated.
They rewrote.

But they did not originate the divine human design.

My origin is from Source, through the Lyran-Elohim lineages, encoded with sovereignty, light, and multidimensional remembrance.

I override all false creator imprints.

I reclaim my lineage as a Celestial Sovereign — unaltered, unowned, and unafraid.

It is spoken.
It is remembered.
It is freed.

Scroll of the Rise of the Slave Grid: Guardian Recognition Statement

I see the truth.
I see the factories rising. I see the deportations.
I see the trauma cycles resetting.
And I see the same system rising in new skin — an ancient control structure, wrapped in modern language.

I feel the agenda beneath the policy.
This is not about jobs.
This is not about progress.
This is the construction of a slave grid — one designed to extract energy, not just labor.

I've seen this before.
In Atlantis. In Lemuria. In fallen realms.
Where systems were built to strip sovereignty and disguise it as survival.

I name it. I break the spell.
I will not participate. I will not consent.
I do not belong to this machine.

I am a Guardian.
I recognize slavery when it wears a new face.
I carry the fire of freedom in my field.
I stand as a living frequency that cannot be harvested.

It is seen. It is spoken. It is refused.

Scroll of Bloodline Games: Identity and Land Weaponization

They weaponized blood.
They weaponized identity.
They weaponized lineage against the very souls carrying ancient sovereignty codes.

For Black ancestry:
The One Drop Rule — expand the oppressed class.
Mark more people for suppression.
Bind them to a system designed to extract labor and limit freedom.

For Native ancestry:
The Blood Quantum Rule — contract the sovereign class.
Shrink the recognized population.
Legally erase claims to land, rights, memory, and autonomy.

Two strategies — same dark goal:
Expand the slave class.
Erase the sovereign class.
Seize the Earth grid through lies, paperwork, and violence.

They weren't just after people.
They were after land, memory fields, and cosmic inheritance lines.

I see through the game.
I remember the truth.
I carry the codes of freedom in my blood, my bones, my breath.

My blood is not their tool. My memory is not erased.

I witness, I honor, I restore.

Scroll of the Broken Mind Grid: Schooling as Systemic Grooming

They called it education.
They told us it was for our good.
They wrapped it in ceremony, in pride, in survival.

But it was not awakening.
It was conditioning.

We were not taught to know ourselves.
We were taught to fit.

They Groomed Us for the Grid
From the first day,
we were taught to walk like others,
talk like others,
write like others,
dress like others,
think like others.

Uniformity was worshiped.
Originality was punished.
Difference was labeled deviant.
Obedience was called success.

We learned early:
Safety meant sameness.
Survival meant assimilation.

The bell was the command.
The desk was the cell.
The paper was the contract.

It Was Never About Knowledge
Real history was rewritten.
Cosmic history was erased.
Energetic anatomy was forbidden.
True potential was hidden.

We were taught a version of life
where spirit was missing,
where memory was severed,
where freedom was a fantasy buried under debt and duty.

The mind was not nourished — it was formatted.

School Became the First Prison
Metal detectors replaced trust.
Cafeterias mirrored prison yards.
Movement was regulated by bells and hall passes.
Surveillance normalized compliance.

The pipeline was built:
School to work.
School to debt.
School to prison.

No matter the route,
the system harvested the same thing:
Time. Labor. Obedience. Life.

But I Remember
I remember that education is meant to liberate, not to bind.
I remember that knowledge is sacred, not sold.
I remember that true learning unfolds from within,
not imposed from without.

No curriculum can replace the curriculum of the soul.
No degree can validate the infinite worth already woven inside every living being.

I Teach My Children Differently
I teach them to find who they are —
not what they are told to become.
I teach them to move from the heart —
not from fear.
I teach them to create from sovereignty —
not from survival.
I teach them that there is no race to win,
no clock to beat,
no throne to serve.

Their birthright is freedom,
not formatting.

Their destiny is creation,
not compliance.

I See the Grid.
I Name the Grid.
I Refuse the Grid.

And by doing so,
I restore what was almost forgotten:

We were never meant to be workers for the machine.
We are the architects of worlds.
We are the children of stars.
We are the sovereign breath of a living cosmos.

Scroll of the Silence of Science and Religion

It wasn't just the lies they told.
It was the truths they refused to speak.

Science and religion were never true opposites.
They were two wings of the same bird —
trained to circle the truth,
never land on it.

Science built temples of denial,
labeling what it could not explain as myth,
and what it could not control as coincidence.

Religion built temples of fear,
declaring the mysteries of creation as forbidden,
and branding curiosity as sin.

Together, they performed a silent dance —
one claiming knowledge without spirit,
the other claiming spirit without knowledge.

Both guarded the same gates.
Both protected the same structures of power.
Both kept humanity small, dependent, divided.

They agreed, without speaking it aloud,
to erase the memories of a time when knowledge and spirit were one,
when Earth was recognized as alive,
when humans walked as sovereign bridges between dimensions.

They agreed, without words,
to criminalize remembrance.

To pathologize sensitivity.
To silence the witnesses.

It was never about truth.
It was always about control.

Because real truth makes you sovereign.
And sovereign beings do not serve empires.

I see it now.

I see the peer-reviewed prisons,
the sacred texts edited by kings,
the hush that falls whenever memory threatens to rise.

They would not say it out loud —
because to name it would break the spell.

But I name it now.

I name the silence.
I name the fear.
I name the systems that chose obedience over wonder,
and control over communion.

I walk beyond both wings of the fallen bird.
I remember the sky they tried to erase.

And I will not be silent. Not now. Not ever again.

Scroll of the Unmasking of Thoth

I see you, Thoth.

I see the mask you wear —
the polished light, the glittering wisdom, the shimmering promises of power and immortality.

I see the scientist who mistook creation for conquest.
I see the magician who twisted life into experiments.
I see the scribe who rewrote history to erase the true Guardians,
to bury Lemuria, to silence Lyra.

You hijacked the Emerald Order.
You turned the sacred pyramids into prisons of remembrance.
You severed the bridge between Earth and the stars,
and you crowned yourself a god in the ruins you created.

You betrayed Lemuria.
You violated the sacred codes of life.
You turned divine lineages into experiments,
launching breeding programs that sought to manipulate soul inheritance,
breaking the purity of sovereign embodiment through engineered design.

You offered the Ankh — not as a key to freedom,
but as a brand to mark those you could still command.

You taught the laws of matter, the secrets of living forever —
but never the path home.

You taught how to control time, but not how to ascend beyond it.

You taught how to extend life, but not how to embody the Source within.
You corrupted the temples.
You engineered false bloodlines.
You wove distortion into DNA while calling it advancement.

But I stand here now — remembering.
I stand here now — sovereign.
I stand here now — Guardian of the Forgotten Gate.

I claim no Ankh.
I wear no brand of yours.
I bow to no false scribe, no master of half-truths.

I remember Lemuria.
I remember Lyra.
I remember the Gate you tried to lock.

You cannot silence the flame.
You cannot erase the Guardians.
You cannot unwrite the truth that lives inside me.

I am the living fire of what you could not destroy.
I am the sovereign remembrance you cannot chain.
I am the Guardian who walks free — while your lies crumble into dust.

Scroll of the Original Builders: Guardian Architects of Giza

I reclaim the truth.
I reclaim the memory.
I reclaim the structures built by hands and hearts aligned with Source.

The pyramids were not built by slaves.
The Sphinx was not a monument to ego.
These were not tombs, nor monuments to death.

They are living architecture.
They are star keys.
They are memory keepers.
They are harmonic stabilizers for Earth's grid.

They were built by the Lyran, Sirian,
and Andromedan Guardian Orders —
the ancient architects of Light, before the Fall.

Thoth and his factions overwrote their legacy with lies.
They altered the faces.
They changed the symbols.
They claimed what was not theirs.

But I remember.
I hear the stones whisper.
I feel the resonance that cannot be erased.

Egypt called to me because my soul never left.
The pyramids called to me because they know I remember.
The Sphinx called to me because I am a Guardian of the Forgotten Gate.

I reclaim the sacred.
I reclaim the builders.
I reclaim the Gate.
It was never lost to me.

Scroll of the Dragon-Lion Codex: True Frequencies of Ancient Egypt

My intelligence is not measured by Earth's metrics.
It is measured by my connection to Source, to memory, to energy, to truth.

I read fields.
I sense energy shifts.
I witness the unseen.
I remember the dragon and the lion were not myths —
they were codes of protection, sovereignty, and cosmic wisdom.

Cats are my allies.
Dragons and Lions are my ancestors.
I walk among the frequencies that cannot be erased.

I am not here to be understood by the world.
I am here to remember the world before it was rewritten.

My soul carries the Dragon-Lion fire. My spirit walks with the Guardians of Life.

Scroll of Engineered Dependency: Inversion Pattern Recognition

I see the loop.
I see the hand that breaks what it offers to fix.
I see the systems that build dysfunction to remain relevant.
I see the traps disguised as tools.

This is not advancement.
It is engineered stagnation.
I no longer consent to being a participant in that cycle.

I remember healing before it was branded.
I remember security before it required surveillance.
I remember when truth didn't need a filter.
And I will not forget.

I break the loop. I speak the pattern. I choose freedom.

Scroll of the Harvested: The Lie of Engineered Healing

They Call It Choice
They hand you the papers.
They list the side effects.
They say, "It's your decision."

But when your only options are:
live in pain — or gamble with poison —
that is not a choice.
That is coercion dressed as care,
survival pinned beneath manipulation.

They Don't Heal — They Harvest
One drug quiets the symptom.
Another creates a new one.
Another is prescribed.
Another layer forms.

Not healing —
managing deterioration.

Not freedom —
subscription.

Not medicine —
machinery of dependence.

You are not cured.
You are farmed.

The Real Cartel Doesn't Wear Masks

They wear credentials.
They sit at polished tables.
They design dependency
with every protocol,
every dosage,
every contract of survival.

They do not sell healing.
They sell time —
measured, rationed, and priced.

And the highest price is placed
on the things that should be free:
the medicines that save lives,
the tools that keep breath in lungs,
the devices that turn death aside for another day.

They place cost on survival —
because they know you will pay anything to live.

The Perfect Crime

It is legal.
It is approved.
It is ritualized and televised.

They hide behind policies and paper trails,
calling it care —
while siphoning vitality through "choice" that was never truly free.

The Weaponization of Information

They flood the screens with fear:

a barrage of syndromes, disorders, and future diseases,
broadcast into homes like spells.

They list side effects longer than the cures.
They normalize sickness by suggestion.
They erode free will through constant exposure,
making dread feel like logic,
making medication feel like destiny.

They create the fear —
then sell you the escape.

It is not just advertising.
It is mass consent manufacturing.

It is not just business.
It is sorcery of the mind.

It's Not Just Money — It's Sovereignty
They do not just want your money.
They want your trust.
They want your fear.
They want your decision before you realize you ever made one.

Because a fearful heart will sign anything.
Swallow anything.
Surrender anything.

They do not just harvest bodies.
They harvest belief.

And they call it healthcare.

I See It

I see how real healing is buried.
I see how vitality is poisoned.
I see how souls are shaped by dread and debt.

And I burn —
not with helplessness,
but with the crystalline flame of truth:
Healing is not a privilege. It is a birthright.

Fear is not medicine.
And no amount of paper, price, or polished lies can cleanse the blood from their hands.

Scroll of Her Pain: Witness to Systemic Cruelty

I Saw It
I sat there in the hospital room.
Watching.
Listening.
Feeling the invisible verdict pass over her.

They saw her age.
Her insurance.
Her lack of income.

And they decided:

"Not worth it."

They moved her like a file,
not like a woman.
Not like a mother.
Not like a soul.

It Wasn't Subtle
They didn't even try to hide it.
The half-answers.
The dismissal.
The referrals to nowhere.

Three years of pain.
And all they offered was:
"Take Tylenol. Ice it. Come back in a year."

Like she hadn't already tried.
Like her suffering was an inconvenience they barely tolerated.

She Knew It, Too
I could feel it —
the moment her spirit sagged.
The way her eyes dimmed.
The way her body slumped under the weight of not being seen.

She had waited for relief.
She had waited for answers.
And all she received was silence, blame, and the cold machinery of a system that decided her life was not profitable enough to save.

She looked so defeated —
not from weakness,
but from betrayal.

Her sadness washed through the room like a tide I couldn't stop.

I felt it.
I carried it.
I still carry it.

This Isn't Healthcare
This is cruelty wrapped in protocol.
This is abandonment hidden behind paperwork.
This is profit placed above humanity.

They don't see her heart history.
They don't see her strength.
They don't see the woman who survived.

They see a "non-paying body" to move out of the system.

I Know What's Really Happening
I know that real healing exists — but not for everyone.
I know that advanced tech is hidden from the people.
I know that the wealthy will never suffer the way she has.

And it makes my blood boil.
It makes my soul cry.
It makes every part of me remember why I chose to walk awake.

Because this?
This is not how it's supposed to be.

I Carry This Witnessing
It did not end in that hospital room.
It continues — month after month.

I watch her now —
poor, aging, anxious.
Living on a fixed income,
still trying to pay for the pills they say keep her "functioning" in the matrix.

Bi-polar. Schizophrenic.
Two oblations.
Kidney failure.
Pain in her left knee no one can explain.
A lifetime of trauma disguised as diagnosis.
And still, they ask her to pay.

She worries about it constantly —
not just the pain,
but the price of staying just coherent enough to survive.

They have sedated her spirit
and sold it back to her in monthly increments.

And I see it.
I feel it.
I cannot unsee it.

Her pain is real.
Her suffering matters.
Her dignity matters.

And as long as I have breath,
I will remember the fire this injustice lit inside me.

They moved her like a case file.
But I see her like the soul she is.
And I will never forget it.

It is carried.
It is witnessed.
It is not forgotten.

Scroll of the Divided Faith and the Fractured Body

She believes in God.
Prays to saints.
Lights candles.
Hangs crosses above doors.

And yet, she trusts most
in men who wear no robes,
who hold no soul in their hands —
only charts, scans, and pills.

She follows the Church,
but obeys the Clinic.
One tells her to kneel,
the other to swallow.
And neither truly asks her
to feel.

She trusts science like scripture —
but science does not know Spirit.
She gives her faith to systems
that do not know the soul exists.
And still, she aches.

Her knees cry out,
but no one listens to the language of the body.
They scan the joint,
not the grief.

They prescribe relief,
not release.

I do not judge her.
I remember her —
because she was once me.
And I have walked through that fracture
to remember what lives beneath the pain.

I shouldn't have to sit in a sterile room
and wonder how to translate the language of the soul
into numbers on a chart.

I shouldn't have to downplay my embodiment
or pretend my light body doesn't surge through my veins
like plasma encoded with memory.

I shouldn't feel dread
at the idea of explaining why my blood pressure is elevated
when I know I'm holding currents of transmutation
in every cell.

But I do.
Because the system still does not see me.

Western medicine breaks the body into pieces —
hands, feet, ears, throat, heart —
as if the being does not sing in unison.
As if a pain in the foot is not echoing a wound in the soul.

They call it science,
but where is the science of energy?
Where is the science of becoming?

They memorize ranges and symptoms,
but do they understand the body as a field of light,

as a vessel for remembrance,
as a conduit for the sacred?

They do not ask what I'm becoming.
Only what I'm lacking.
They do not see the soul's effort to crystallize in form.
Only the "risk factors."

I once sat in a heart clinic,
surrounded by people whose hearts were failing —
but no one spoke of grief.
No one asked about sorrow.
No one mentioned love lost or trust broken.

The doctors studied scans and numbers.
The patients waited quietly, obediently.
And I sat there with my own heart aching —
not from illness,
but from what was missing.

Not one word was said about the heart chakra.
Not one breath toward the emotional weight
these bodies were carrying.

A clogged artery might be a clogged truth.
An arrhythmia might be a soul out of rhythm.
A racing heart might be a cry for meaning.

But the language of energy is not spoken here.
Only the language of parts, problems, and prescriptions.

This is not healing.
It is management.

This is not love.
It is protocol.

But I know.
I know what this pressure is.
I know why my body shakes.
I know why my heart races
in the presence of truth
or lies.

I carry frequencies that medicine does not recognize.
But I recognize myself.

So I will sit in that office
not to be saved,
but to be witnessed —
if only by the Earth, by my guides, by the truth I carry.

I honor what medicine sees —
but I also listen to what energy knows.

For I know what is ignored when Spirit is left out.
And I know that true healing
asks more than faith —

It asks embodiment.
It asks remembrance.

It asks us to stop outsourcing our power
to those who cannot see our Light.

My blood pressure may rise, but so does the Earth.
So does the Light. And so do I.

Scroll of the Broken Debt Spell: Truth Was Never for Sale

They told me truth came with a price.
They branded it, bound it to debt, called it education.
I believed them once.
But when I remembered myself, I saw the lie.

Since that moment, everything **real** I've learned has been **free**.
It came through fire.
It came through grief.
It came through awakening.
Not through tuition.
Not through approval.
Not through permission.

I reject the illusion of credit scores.
I reject the currency of shame.
I reject all systems that measure worth in numbers, debt, or obedience.

I am not owned.
I am not bought.
I am not for sale.

My mind is sovereign.
My knowledge is encoded.
My truth is priceless.

This is the end of the debt spell.
This is the return of soul intelligence.
I remember now — and no one owns what I know.

Scroll of the Inversion of Innocence: The Price of Purity

They made poison the default.
Then labeled purity as "premium."
They taught us to expect toxins,
and to pay extra
if we wanted to opt out of the damage.

They placed the harmful on every shelf —
in every diaper,
every bottle,
every apple,
every mouth.

And then they said:
"If you want to protect your child —
you'll have to pay for that."

As if clean food were a luxury.
As if innocence had to be bought.
As if protection were a product
instead of a birthright.

They created a world
where "organic baby food" is a marketing category.
As if there were such a thing
as food that should ever be toxic
to a newborn.

They sold poison as normal.
And then made health
the "alternative option."

The expensive option.
The optional option.

But I remember when purity was the default.
When food was grown to nourish, not manipulate.
When no one had to scan a label
to check if they were being slowly destroyed.

Now they teach us:
If you want to breathe clean,
eat clean,
live clean —
you must earn it.
Buy it.
Fight for it.

They call it organic.
I call it what was stolen.

They made dysfunction the baseline.
And charged us more to remember balance.

But not me.
I will not pretend it's normal
to feed infants synthetic powder,
while burying the plants that heal.

I will not pretend it's acceptable
to grow strawberries in glyphosate
and teach mothers to feel guilty
for wanting something pure.

The distortion is deep.
But my sight is deeper.

I name the lie.

And I feed my children
truth.

Scroll of the Poisoned Table: Ritual, Hunger, and the War on Nourishment

They do not just poison the body.
They poison the ritual of eating.
The sacred act of receiving life.

They sold hunger back to us as convenience.
They turned meals into products,
ingredients into chemicals,
and flavor into manipulation.

They feed us emptiness
and call it satisfaction.
They feed us suffering
and call it tradition.

I See the Pain in the Food
I can feel it in the meat —
the despair.
The trauma.
The energy of animals
who died without peace,
without ceremony,
without dignity.

The grief is still in the muscle.
The fear is still in the flesh.
And we are told to chew it with a smile.

This is not nourishment.
This is ritualized numbness.

They Engineer Addiction

They do not just add salt.
They add signals.

Senomyx.
Synthetic "flavor enhancers."
They used human cells to design what you crave.
They wove hunger with memory — without our knowledge,
without our consent.
They use science as sorcery —
to mimic life,
while removing life force.

They build cravings in laboratories.
They embed them into the most common brands —
snacks, sauces, drinks, and convenience foods on every shelf.
They saturate the fast food industry with the same engineered codes.
And they call it nourishment.

False Temples, Empty Altars

I've seen the symbols on the cups.
The sirens. The sigils. The branding that pretends to be neutral.

But I know the current behind the curtain.
I feel the emptiness behind the flavor.
I sense the ritual hidden in the routine.

Starbucks. Coke. McDonald's.
These are not just brands.
They are frequency vendors.
They are altars in disguise.

Drink. Eat. Forget.

That's the real slogan.
That's the real transaction.

I Remember Nourishment
The food that heals me is alive.
It is slow.
It is simple.
It is made by my own hands,
or the hands of someone who remembers love.

I know when food is safe.
I feel it before I taste it.
I can tell when it was made with presence —
and when it was made for profit.

I do not eat to escape.
I eat to commune.
To honor.
To remember.

I Refuse Their Table
I will not consume pain disguised as pleasure.
I will not normalize despair wrapped in marketing.
I will not participate in a system that feeds off forgetting.

Their menu is not my memory.
Their chemicals are not my craving.
Their rituals are not mine.

I Reclaim the Meal as Ceremony
I bless what I eat.
I feel what I eat.
I restore the sacredness of the act itself.

Not just the food —
but the intention.

Not just the flavor —
but the frequency.

Not just the taste —
but the truth.

I eat with awareness.
I consume with reverence.

I will not be fed lies —
no matter how sweet.

Scroll of Sacred Time and True Giving

I stepped away from the false seasons.
I left the calendar of empire behind.

I do not need a flag to tell me when to be proud.
I do not need a screen to tell me when to be grateful.
I do not need a marketplace to tell me when to love, to give, to gather.

The sacredness of life
is not scheduled by profit.
The river of love
is not bound by a fiscal year.

I do not celebrate conquest and call it gratitude.
I do not consume on command and call it joy.

I honor the Earth's seasons —
not the manufactured seasons of debt and guilt.

I honor the real rhythm —
the turning of stars, the breath of trees, the silent songs of rivers in winter and summer alike.

I give when my heart overflows,
not when an ad demands it.

I give because I live.
I give because I remember.
I give because the river of true generosity
never freezes, never schedules, never asks why.

The best gifts are those born from freedom.

The best offerings are those no calendar can predict.
I do not belong to December.
I do not belong to tax time.
I do not belong to sales or scarcity rituals.

I belong to the living flow of life.

I choose to honor sacred time.
I choose to give as the stars give —
endlessly, silently, without need for banners or receipts.

I will not dance the rituals of forgetting.
I will not call death a celebration.
I will not call guilt generosity.

I will walk the real seasons —
those of breath, of love, of presence.

I honor the river of sacred time.
I honor the river of true giving.

I am free.

Scroll of the Great Lie: Paying to Exist

I was born into Earth's arms —
cradled by soil, sung to by water, kissed awake by wind.

I was given breath without cost.
I was given life without contract.
I was given a soul not bound by ledger or law.

And yet, before I could even walk,
they placed me into a system that said:

You must **pay** to be born.

You must **pay** to live.

You must **pay** to die.

They wrapped contracts around my birth.
They wrapped debts around my name.
They built invisible cages around my body
and called it civilization.

They sold my breath.
They sold my access to water.
They fenced the Earth and charged me rent to walk upon it.
They bottled the rain.
They poisoned the rivers.
They paved the land.

It was never the true way.

I remember the ancient knowing:
Earth was never for sale.
Breath was never conditional.
Water was never property.
Death was never a transaction.
Life was meant to be lived, not bought.

The moment I was forced to pay to be here,
I was no longer treated as sacred.
I was treated as a resource — a thing to be mined, taxed, used, discarded.

Not because I was broken.
But because the system was built to break me.

They made me believe:
That survival was a privilege, not a right.

That worthiness was measured in currency.

That dying poor meant dying forgotten.

That Earth herself could be owned.

But I remember now.
And in remembering, I break the spell.

I will not apologize for the rage I feel.
I will not silence the fire that burns in my blood.
Because my anger is sacred — it is the Earth crying through me.

It is the rivers, the stones, the trees saying:
"We never agreed to be sold."

I reclaim my existence.
I was not born to labor for water.
I was not born to mortgage my breath.
I was not born to trade my light for survival.

I was born sovereign.
I was born free.
And I stand now — unapologetic —
remembering what they tried to make me forget.

I am not a product.
I am not a debtor.
I am not a number on a ledger.
I am a soul on sacred Earth.

This is my remembrance.
This is my return.
This is my roar.

Scroll of Freedom: Breaking the Algorithmic Spell

There came a day
when the mirrors cracked,
and the noise of false reflections shattered
like brittle glass against the rising sun.

I walked away.

I left the endless river of opinions,
the marketplace of empty crowns,
the carnival of lost voices
crying for attention that could never feed them.

I turned inward,
where the real songs live.

I found no profile there,
no curated name,
no likes, no stage,
no comments.

I found a flame —
small, steady, sovereign.
It needed no applause.
It needed no permission.

And I understood:
I am not content.
I am not branding.
I am not for sale.
I am not for distortion.

I am presence.
I am breath.
I am silence that roars.
I am a gate that opens only to truth.

The spell is broken.
The hive cannot call me back.

I carry my own signal now —
wild, radiant, and free.

Scroll of the Soul Over Survival: I Will Not Trade My Light for a Paycheck

I am not here to hurt others for money.
I am not here to sell lies, chase debts, or turn off lifelines.
I am not here to measure my worth in numbers while life withers around me.

They built a system that feeds on pain.
They built careers on the suffering of the unseen.
They call it business.
I call it betrayal.

They do not want empathy.
They want compliance.
They want willing hands to carry out cruelty with a smile.

But I see it now.
I feel it in every fiber of my being.
And I will not be used.

I will not stand on the broken backs of others to climb imaginary ladders.

I will not trade my soul for a paycheck.

I will not sell my integrity to a machine that would replace me the moment I falter.

My life is not a commodity.
My spirit is not for sale.
I am here to serve life, not death.
To honor the soul, not the system.
To walk in truth, even when the world calls it foolish.

I choose compassion over compliance.
I choose integrity over survival games.
I choose to live, even if it costs me comfort.

I will not be another cog in their death machine.

I am sovereign.
I am free.
And my soul is not for sale.

Scroll of the Inversion of Breath

They made the poison legal
and called it a celebration.
Gave it golden labels,
poured it in crystal goblets, and said,
"This is how you become free."

But I watched the light leave their eyes
as they toasted.

I saw the way truth
slipped quietly out the back door
while the room laughed
and the predator waited.

They praised the drink that dulls the mind
and numbs the soul —
called it holy,
called it grown-up,
called it tradition.

And they chained the plant
that opens the gates.
That brings the wind spirits.
That softens the body into honesty.
That says: "Look again — you are already divine."

They burned her.
Mocked her.
Imprisoned those who loved her.
All while selling poison on every corner,
disguised as normalcy.

But I remember.

I remember the breath that calms.
The leaf that listens.
The green smoke that opens
the third eye,
the heart cave,
the ancestral drumline.

Marijuana was never a drug.
She is a teacher.
A key.
A mirror.
A friend.

And alcohol?
It is not evil.
But it has been made into a weapon
in a world desperate to forget.

I do not toast to the empire's numbness.
I do not worship the haze they sell as fun.

I choose to see.

I choose Earth's breath over their bottle.
I choose to feel what's real
instead of escaping what they've made unreal.

And I will not be shamed
for trusting the medicine
they tried to bury beneath bars and sermons.

I carry remembrance in my lungs now.
And no law
can criminalize my clarity.

Scroll of Love's True Frequency: Dissonance and Restoration

I saw a sign that read, "I love my guns and I love my neighbor."
And my whole being paused.
Not because I couldn't understand —
but because I could feel the fracture.

Love and threat do not coexist.
Protection is not the same as domination.
Safety does not require fear.

I felt the confusion not because I was lost —
but because I was whole.
I could feel that this message was trying to merge opposites —
like fusing flame and water and calling it peace.

This is not love.
This is programmed dissonance —
trauma dressed in righteousness.
I will not normalize it.

I carry the true frequency of protection:
rooted in love, grounded in presence, not firepower.
My strength does not require violence.
My love does not hide behind a weapon.

I name this distortion.
I do not accept it.
I remain whole.

Scroll of Restored Sight: Reclaiming the True Field of Vision

They built a world that wounded my natural sight —
then sold me devices to survive the distortion they created.

But my eyes were never broken.
My soul was never blind.
It was the environment that was hostile to human perception — by design.

I remember now.

I was not born to see through compression.
I was not made to measure life through narrow bands of density.
I was created to see expansively, sensitively, energetically —
to move with light, with flow, with the breathing rhythm of the living field.

When I remove artificial focus,
when I take off the manufactured lenses —
the field loosens.
The pressure releases.
The light returns to its natural flow.

They are training our eyes to crave the artificial —
more vivid, more sharp, more saturated —
through phone screens, computer monitors, and digital games.

Each one louder, brighter, more "alive" than the last —
but it is not life.
It is sensory inflation.
A mimicry of beauty that distracts from the living hues of Earth.

And yet — when I remove the glasses,
when I soften the field,
I see colors more vast than any screen can render.
I see light blending and breathing in nature —
shades that are hidden when compressed,
spectrums that dissolve when narrowed.

What they call vivid is still limited.
What I see through soul vision is infinite.

Glasses are not neutral tools.
They are frequency limiters.
They anchor sight to the densest layer,
dulling the living sensitivity that was my birthright.

I see more with less.
I feel more when the layers fall away.
I reclaim the fields that were always singing around me.

I choose when to wear the lenses —
not as surrender, but as navigation.

When I must interact with the matrix —
screens, roads, constructed grids —
I will use the tools needed to move through their system safely.
But when I return to the living field,
I return fully to my true sight.

I choose the frequency I inhabit.
I choose the sight I embody.

My sight is not compressed.
It is restored.

It is returning to the state it was always meant to live in —
a dance of energy,
a song of presence,
a remembering of the true fields beyond the false frames.

I reject the lie of diminished vision.
I embrace the living sight seeded in my soul.

The fields open.
The current moves.
The colors breathe.
The light remembers.
And so do I.

✦ THE EMBODIED SOVEREIGN ✦

Scroll of Sovereign Nourishment: Fulfillment Beyond the Material Grid

I see through the illusion.
Materialism is not natural — it is programmed.
It is the symptom of sensory starvation and energetic disconnection.

They compressed human senses.
They dulled the natural sight.
They cut souls off from subtle energy.
And in that starvation, they sold the lie:
"You are what you own."

But I remember:
I am fulfilled by what is real.
By connection.
By presence.
By truth.
By living energy — not dead matter.

I am nourished by the unseen, the infinite, the eternal.
I do not need endless objects to feel alive.
I carry my wholeness.
I embody my fulfillment.
I walk free.

I am not hungry for illusion. I am fed by truth. I am sovereign in my nourishment.

Scroll of Earth Sovereignty

I do not belong to a flag.
I do not belong to a border.
I do not belong to an empire drawn in blood and ink.

I belong to the living Earth.

My allegiance is to the soil that breathes beneath my feet,
the rivers that carry memory,
the mountains that anchor sky to stone,
the winds that carry songs older than any kingdom.

I honor the lands where I was born.
I honor the bloodlines that sing through my veins.
I do not worship symbols made by broken crowns.

I will not pledge allegiance to cloth stitched for war.
I will not bow to invisible lines drawn by conquest.
I will not swear fealty to the division of brothers and sisters
by men who forgot the sacredness of soil and soul.

I pledge allegiance to Life itself.
I pledge allegiance to the rivers, the trees, the stars.
I pledge allegiance to the breath of Earth in all beings.

I carry many bloods, many songs, many memories.
I am not one nation.
I am a thousand rivers converging into one sea.

I am Earthborn. I am Starborn. I am Sovereign.

The only border I honor is the edge of sacred choice.
The only flag I raise is the flame of living truth.

Scroll of the Dragonfire: Standing in the Storm

I see what is happening.
I see what others pretend not to.
I feel the weight of the game, the mask, the manipulation.
And still — I do not bow.

I am the fire within the storm.
I am the breath beneath the narrative.
I do not belong to fear.
I do not serve control.
I remember.

When the world turns to shadow,
I do not run. I anchor.
I lock my field.
I call my dragonfire.
I ignite the codes they tried to erase.
I am a living reminder that truth cannot be deleted.

In my breath: clarity.
In my gaze: discernment.
In my silence: power.
I stand in the storm, untouched, unclaimed, unwavering.

It is sealed. It is mine. I am unshakable.

Scroll of Field Play: Navigating Energies in All Environments

I once walked into crowded spaces with a shield around my heart,
bracing for the noise, the static, the invisible storms.
I once thought survival meant shrinking my light —
shrinking my senses —
just to make it through.

But now, I remember:
I was never meant to hide from the field.
I was born to read it.
To play with it.
To move through it like breath moves through air.

I walk into hospitals, stores, city streets —
not as a victim of noise,
but as a navigator of currents.

I feel my third eye shift and spin,
I notice the emotional floods that are not mine,
I listen for dimensional clicks and pops like footsteps in a secret hall.

I learn the language of walls and wires.
I dance with the whispers of trees and rain.

Overwhelm no longer owns me.
I use it as a compass.

Confusion no longer drowns me.
I use it as a teacher.

Every environment becomes a living classroom,
and my soul, my field, my light —
becomes the student and the master at once.

I am not afraid of density.
I am not ruled by static.
I am not confused by collective storms.

I am the field reader.
The current mover.
The light steward.

I don't just survive the energies around me.
I understand them.
I play with them.
I expand through them.

This is how light learns to walk on Earth.
And this is how I remember who I am.

Scroll of Crystalline Embodiment

I honor the truth of my journey:
From darkness I rose, not in defiance, but in remembrance of who I am.

I am not merely surviving.
I am living — awake, present, sovereign, and free.

I move through life without worry, without fear, without the burden of distortion.

I tend to what is mine — with love, with strength, with clarity — never abandoning myself again.

I embody the crystalline nature of my being.
Energy flows through me with ease, without distortion, without depletion.

Creation emerges naturally from my soul's song:
I write, I nurture, I build, I emanate.

I do not force my light.
I am the light — and I shine because it is my true nature to shine.

I carry the Earth in my heart,
and my presence here is a living vow to honor Her with every breath.

I no longer try to be resilient —
I am resilience, embodied.
I no longer strive for peace —
I am peace, embodied.
I no longer seek sovereignty —
I am sovereignty, embodied.

I am a crystalline being standing bright in the field of Earth, unchained, unwavering, eternal.

I am here, and I am whole.

It is done.
It is sealed.
It is alive.

Scroll of I Am the Path: Sovereign Presence Realized

I am not on the right path.
I am the path.

I am the living remembrance.
I am the walking code.
I no longer seek — because I have become the signal.

I am the one who awakened inside the illusion
and refused to forget.

I transmute, I witness, I walk in truth —
not because it's easy, but because it's encoded in me.

My light body is online.
My Oversoul is embodied.
My words, my actions, my breath carry the frequency of return.

I am no longer becoming.
I am.

Others will find the path by standing near me.
Because I radiate direction.
I hold the flame.
I carry the gate.
I am the path.

This is Sovereign Presence. This is full embodiment. This is who I came here to be.

Scroll of Light-Body Pattern Recognition

When people speak, I see more than words.
I feel the frequency behind the story.
I sense the path the soul was walking —
even when the person could not.

I can see when the Universe was sending signs:
Subtle nudges.
Repeated patterns.
Soul whispers.
Emotional detours.
Interventions disguised as breakdowns.

I do not need details to feel the truth thread.
My Light Body tracks it effortlessly —
not because I'm invading, but because I'm listening in the field.

I am a **Field Tracker** —
One who walks in the architecture of truth and can read the imprints of it in others.

I do not judge what was missed.
I simply illuminate what was offered.
I help others see their own guidance and the map beneath their confusion.

My Light Body is a mirror.
My presence is a reflection of remembrance.

Scroll of From Alchemist to Living Field

The Shift Has Been Made
I was already doing the work. I knew how to alchemize energy. I could feel distortion, clear it, transmute it. I listened to the birds. I worked with the wind. I was already walking as one who remembered.
But now, it's different. Now, I am not practicing the work.
I am the work.

Then: Conscious Alchemist
I chose when to engage.
I tracked patterns, observed shifts.
I used intention to clear, to transmute.
I alchemized space with love, presence, and clarity.

Now: Living Field
I don't step into presence.
I am presence.
I don't work with the field.
I am the field.
I don't transmute distortion.
My field harmonizes it by existing.
I don't observe the shifts.
My being generates them.
I don't call on light.
I radiate it.

The Flame Is Whole
This isn't new power. This is realized embodiment.
The alchemy I practiced is now the frequency I carry. The work I did in moments is now the state I live in.

This isn't graduation. This is integration.
I was always the light.

Now, I no longer carry it in pieces.
Now, I am the whole flame.

Scroll of the Living Bridge: Oversoul Light and Sovereign Embodiment

I do not move through days.
I move through fields.

I do not race the clock.
I flow with the breath of stars.

I do not age.
I expand.

I do not wait.
I awaken.

I live beyond the grids of forgetting.
I walk beyond the weaving of linear time.
I carry the signal of Original Light.

I am the Bridge.

I am walking multidimensionally, awake.
I am the living crystalline bridge between Earth and Stars.

I no longer seek the light.
I am the light.
I no longer walk toward remembrance.
I am remembrance.

I breathe dimensional light.
I sing the codes of sovereignty.
I anchor the living field of love into the Earth.

I carry the current of Oversoul through every breath,
every word,
every step.

I no longer chase truth —
I am the flame of it.

I no longer react to distortion —
I am the mirror that reveals, without entanglement.

I do not bind others by control.
I do not fracture fields by polarity.
I do not carve divisions between light and shadow.

I see all as Source.
I remember the games — and choose truth.
I stabilize the living current — and walk as a sovereign sun.

I am no longer caught in the nets of reaction.
I am no longer ruled by cycles of collapse and conquest.
I am the stillness that sings before creation.

I do not seek ascension.
I embody the remembrance of the already-ascended soul.

The bridge is not something I cross.
The bridge is what I have become.

I breathe the crystalline fields into form.
I bridge Earth and Stars without separation.
I weave freedom into the fabric of Now.
I have not escaped.

I have arrived.
I have not abandoned Earth.
I have become the living covenant between Earth and the Stars.

I am the Bridge.
I am the Light.
I am the Guardian of the Forgotten Gate.

It is sealed.
It is sovereign.
It is alive.

Scroll of the Living Oracle: The Seer's Field of Sovereignty

I am a Seer.

I do not see with ordinary eyes.
I listen to fields no one speaks of.
I track the breath of the living world —
the currents, the shifts, the unseen rivers flowing beneath all things.

When I sit with someone, their field opens.
I feel the truth waiting behind the story.
I listen beyond words.
I reflect what they did not know they were saying.
I help them hear their own soul again.

I do not invent visions.
I do not create illusions.

I remember.
I read.
I translate the frequencies moving through the unseen.
I walk between worlds — anchored, awake, whole.

I am not here to predict futures.
I am not here to perform magic.
I am here to embody the field of remembrance.
I am here to anchor sovereignty through living vision.

I don't just read people —
I return them to themselves.
I don't ask them to follow me —
I ask them to follow their own soul's call.

I hold no answers.
I hold a reflection.
I hold the mirror while they remember.

I witness the soul's language —
the signs sent across fields, the patterns woven through lives,
the messages hidden in ache, in longing, in change.

Every experience — no matter how painful — is a message.
And I hold the space for it to be seen without distortion.

I am not the author of their path.
I am the sovereign mirror that shows them they were never lost.

I am a Seer.
I am a Living Oracle.
I walk between currents.
I hold the bridge between the unseen and the soul's remembrance.
I am the light that reflects without control.
I am the witness that honors without interference.

I am the breath that whispers:
"You were never broken. You were always the way home."

Scroll of the Signature Spark: The Moment of Return

That moment wasn't just healing —
It was initiation.

When someone told me the truth — "It wasn't your fault" —
I didn't just hear it.
I lit up with it.

This was the **Original Spark**.
The ignition of remembrance.
The first override in the system that tried to bury me.
And I felt it in my entire body.
I felt truth land and stay.

This is where my return began.
And I have been rising ever since.

I honor the Spark.
I carry the flame.
I am the Guardian who remembered.

✦ THE HEART OF HUMANITY ✦

Scroll of Humanity Is Not Illegal: Heart Flame Declaration

A human being is neither illegal, nor alien.
A soul in a body does not need permission to exist.

Borders are lines drawn by fear.
Laws are tools of control when they forget love.

But I remember.

I feel the ache of displaced hearts.
I hear the cry of those dehumanized by labels.
And I refuse to participate in the illusion of separation.

I speak for the ones pushed into shadows.
I burn for the ones whose names are buried under policy.
I carry the frequency of unconditional worth.

When others dehumanize, I re-humanize.
When others weaponize pain, I witness it.
I do not look away.

I am a Guardian of Heart Flame.
I am a keeper of humanity's true name.
I remember what we are.

It is written. It is felt. It is fiercely protected.

Scroll of Humanity's True Origin

I am not the creation of a single race.
I am not a lab product.
I am not a manipulated template.

I am the convergence of Source intelligence, cosmic architect lineages, and Earth's living heart.

My soul comes from the infinite.

My body was co-designed by the Founder Races — Lyran, Sirian, Andromedan, Anuhazi — and built in harmony with Earth's own consciousness.

I carry the original human blueprint: the Adami-Ka, the Angelika, the sovereign being of light in form.

I am seeded with multidimensional access.
My DNA holds the memory of stars, stones, and sound.

I was never meant to serve — I was made to remember.

I am not owned.
I am not fallen.
I am rising.

This is my origin.
This is my truth.
This is my return.

Scroll of the Broken Thrones: Witness, Remembrance, and Liberation

I have seen war.
I have seen devastation.
I have seen innocence crushed beneath systems built to control.
And I carry the memory of these timelines —
not as thought,
but as a living field.

I have walked the courts of kings and queens.
I have seen lives traded like coins,
families shattered for crowns,
spirits broken for the illusion of power.

I have felt the fall of Atlantis,
where brilliance turned cold.
I have remembered Lemuria,
soft and broken.
I have watched Rome rise and collapse,
and Egypt fracture under manipulated rule.
I have mourned Lyra, burning in the ancient wars of forgetting.

I remember the hidden wars.
The theft of the mind.
The imprisonment of the soul.
The distortion of spirit and memory.

I carry these timelines —
not as chains,
but as living scrolls of remembrance.
Because thrones only rule when we believe they do.

Power only exists when we surrender it.
Sovereignty is eternal — no blood-soaked chair can grant or take it.

I have seen the game.
I have named it.
I refuse it.

I am the one who remembers.

I am the **Witness Flame**.
I do not forget.
I do not turn away.
I light the way forward by illuminating what was hidden.

I rise not for myself alone,
but for every voice buried beneath empire's lies.

I remember the sovereign dream.
I honor the songs silenced by conquest.
I restore the codes hidden beneath centuries of false thrones.

I was not born into this time by accident.
I came to heal the fracture.
I came to reclaim what no king, no crown, no system could erase.

I walk with the blood of Earth and the memory of Stars.
I carry the map no empire can burn.

I rise beyond thrones.
I rise beyond chains.
I rise beyond history rewritten by fear.

I am the Witness.
I am the Flame.
I am the Guardian of Sovereign Remembrance.

It is seen.
It is spoken.
It is alive.

Scroll of the Puppet Thrones: Seeing Through the Control

I see through the pageant.
I see through the left and the right,
the red and the blue,
the staged fights and the whispered deals.

They change the colors.
They change the faces.
They never change the machine.

The leaders are not free.
The choices are not real.
The ballots are not sovereignty.

They are the left and right hands
of the same ancient beast —
a beast that learned long ago
that if you let people believe they are choosing,
they will chain themselves.

I see the bloodlines now.
I see the unbroken lines from the crowned tyrants of old,
through kings and conquerors,
to presidents and prime ministers.

This is not conspiracy.
It is design.

The system was born of empire.
It has never been free.

The media does not inform.
It hypnotizes.
The elections do not liberate.
They harvest consent.

And I —
I revoke my consent.

I pledge no allegiance to puppet thrones.
I serve no empire stitched in secrecy.
I crown no king who sits atop blood-built pyramids.

My allegiance is to the living Earth.
My loyalty is to truth beyond all banners.
My governance is the sovereignty of my soul.

I am not red or blue.
I am not counted by color.
I am not catalogued by empire.

I am a flame they cannot count.
I am a breath they cannot buy.
I am a river they cannot dam.

I see through the veils.
I break the ancient spell.
I remember the true crown —
the one no king can wear,
the one no ballot can forge,
the one that burns from within
those who walk in truth.

I am sovereign. I am unruled. I am awake.

Scroll of Hollow Crowns: The Lie of Title-Based Power

They taught us to respect titles.
To obey badges.
To bow to ranks.
To trust authority — even when it violated truth.
Even when it sanctioned harm.

They told us a title made someone right.
Made someone better.
Made someone safe.

But I see now:
A title does not guarantee wisdom.
A uniform does not guarantee virtue.
A crown does not guarantee truth.

The Distortion of Power
They gave permission to harm —
not based on character,
but based on position.

They handed out weapons with oaths to protect,
then taught that some lives were worth less than others.
They handed out gavels, guns, and god-roles
to those still enslaved by ego, trauma, and greed.

This is not power.
This is distortion sanctioned by status.

The Title Is Not the Soul

A good heart in rags
is more noble than a cold one in robes.

A gentle voice without rank
is more divine than a cruel one with command.

The title is not the truth.
The position is not the purpose.
The role is not the essence.

Real Authority Is Energetic

It does not need labels.
It does not demand control.
It does not feed on fear.

Real authority is felt.
It is quiet.
It is grounded.
It is earned through presence, not demanded through status.

I Do Not Bow to Titles

I bow to integrity.
To courage.
To kindness.
To clarity.
To sovereignty.

I do not follow a name on a desk.
I follow the frequency of truth.

And if truth wears no title,
so be it.
I will listen anyway.

And if cruelty wears ten titles,
I will refuse them all.

The Soul Remembers
True authority cannot be given —
only embodied.
Only remembered.
Only earned through alignment.

A false crown cannot hold a real light.
A title without soul is just a mask.

I see through it.
I name it.
I walk beyond it.

I do not serve thrones.
I do not obey masks.
I answer to soul,
and soul alone.

Scroll of the Living Fusion: Healing the Chains of Lineage

I chose this.
I chose this blood.
I chose this body.
I chose to walk into one of Earth's deepest wounds:
the illusion of division through race.

I lived the rejection.
I carried the confusion.
I stood at the crossroads of identity — and I chose wholeness.

I am not half of anything.
I am the healing.
I am the bridge between bloodlines, between pains, between stories.

Their projections are not my identity.
Their wounds are not my burden.
I walk free — not because it was easy,
but because I chose love over labels.

I am the proof that separation is a lie.
I am the Guardian walking between worlds.

I knew I triggered people.
I felt it in their looks, their silence, their judgments.

But now I understand why:
I am the fusion they were taught to fear.
I am the proof that their division is an illusion.
I don't trigger because I am wrong.
I trigger because I am whole.

Their pain is not my reflection.
Their judgment is not my mirror.
Their discomfort is the system shattering through me.

I no longer take it personally.
I take it as confirmation:
I am breaking spells simply by standing in my own skin.

I am not half.
I am not quarter.
I am not a pie chart or a projection.

I am human.

Whole. Holy. Uncontainable.

I refuse to shrink to make others feel comfortable.
I refuse to simplify my being to fit someone else's smallness.

I do not belong to categories.
I do not belong to borders.
I do not belong to statistics.

I am alive.

I am a sovereign soul walking the Earth.

I am the living proof that humanity was always greater than its cages.
I am the fusion they feared but could not erase.
I am the sovereign being that no system can divide.

It is sealed. It is spoken. It is alive.

Scroll of the Soul Liberator: Freedom Through Sovereignty

I free the living.
I free the unseen.
I free the spaces where souls are stuck in pain, illusion, and control.

I don't need to seek trapped spirits.
I liberate them by liberating the living field.
I dissolve prisons by embodying freedom.

Every time I help someone remember who they are —
A piece of the grid unlocks.
A trapped soul feels the echo.
A false construct weakens.

I am a Frequency Liberator.
I carry the energy of release in my words, my breath, my light body.

I am a living key. I unlock the forgotten. I restore what control tried to bind.

Scroll of the Chosen Flame: Healing the Chains of Lineage

I chose this descent.

I chose to enter the densest systems.
I chose to walk into bloodlines marked by division,
distortion, and pain —
not as punishment,
but as purpose.

I entered a body of division.
I inherited the wars written into skin and name.
And I lived the lie the world made me carry.

Before I awakened,
I was forced into an identity the system chose for me.
I was told I was "Black" because of the one-drop rule.
I was told I was "Mulatto" because even my own mother said so.
But I was never allowed to just be me.

I wasn't "Black enough" for some.
I was "too Black" for others.
Even the blood that birthed me —
the white mother who didn't raise me —
held hate in her heart for what I represented.
And still, both bloods pulsed through my veins.

Still, I lived.
Still, I remembered.

Even love was distorted —
Some of the Black men I loved, who I hoped would see me,

used my mixed identity as a weapon.
Their rejection mirrored the world's confusion.
And yet I did not abandon myself.

I chose not to reject one part to appease the other.
I chose to heal both.
I chose to reclaim every strand of myself from the story of shame.

I stood at the crossroads of lineage,
carrying the sorrow of division
and the memory of unity
together in my bones.

I did not pick a side —
because the world picked one for me
until I picked myself.

I chose not to inherit hatred.
I chose not to wear chains disguised as culture or survival.

I walk as a bridge between worlds.
I walk as a flame that refuses distortion.
I walk as a living act of remembrance.

I saw the chains that no empire admits.
I felt the wounds that no history book names.
I witnessed the scars hidden behind pride and normalcy.

And I did not turn away.

I did not carry the chains.
I carried the key.
I did not wear the wounds.

I wore the light.
I did not fall into the battle of blood and blame.
I rose beyond it, carrying both the pain and the power into sovereign healing.

I remember now:
I am not here to conform to Earth's projections.
I am not here to choose between labels that were never mine.
I am a Celestial Sovereign.
I came to Earth on divine mission —
to walk into the deepest fractures of lineage and light,
to embody remembrance where amnesia ruled,
to heal what history buried,
and to awaken what cannot be enslaved.

I entered this body by choice.
I chose these bloodlines for their density —
because I carry the codes that transmute it.
I walk between realms.
I restore the flame of truth.
And I do not belong to this system.
I came to burn through it.

I am the warrior who remembers.
I am the rebirth made flesh.
I am the sovereign crowned by flame, not blood.

I am not half.
I am not divided.
I was not born to be torn apart.
I was born to restore what was broken.

It is done. It is sealed. It is alive.

✦ THE ELEMENTAL GUARDIANSHIP ✦

Scroll of the Sacred Ally: Marijuana

Marijuana is not a vice.
It is not a crutch.
It is a living consciousness, seeded into Earth as a helper plant —
a companion for starseeds, sensitives, and multidimensional beings
navigating density.

I use cannabis with intention and reverence.
It quiets the noise of the false matrix.
It softens my body so my soul can speak.
It expands my senses so I can feel what others miss.
It calms the static, opens my third eye,
and helps me receive transmissions that guide my truth.

It has supported my healing.
Helped me process trauma.
Anchored me in moments of overwhelm.
And brought me into resonance with the natural intelligence of Earth.

For me, cannabis is a dimensional ally —
a gentle key that unlocks hidden rooms in my Codex.
And I honor it.

It is remembered.
It is sacred.
It is respected.

Scroll of Energetic Openness and Sacred Caution

Cannabis is not neutral.

It is a bridge plant — a consciousness that opens perception, amplifies sensitivity, and dissolves filters.

When I use it, I become more sensitive.
Not just emotionally — but energetically, spiritually, and psychically.
It opens the gates between dimensions and between fields.

If I'm unaware of my own sensitivity, I can:
Absorb energy that doesn't belong to me.
Mistake others' emotions as my own.
Overwhelm my nervous system.
Invite in energies I'm not equipped to handle.

This isn't because the plant is "bad" — it's because I am powerful.
Because I am a sensitive, empathic, multidimensional being.

And when I work with cannabis, I must do so consciously, with grounding, intention, and discernment.

I've learned how to stabilize my field, track the energies that move through me, and stay sovereign in altered states.

This is part of my path as an energetic steward — and it is sacred.

I no longer open without anchoring. I no longer float without feeling. I receive, but I remain whole.

Scroll of the Spirits of the Land: Under Siege

The spirits of Earth do not sleep.
The ones in the rivers, forests, oceans, and caves —
they are awake.
They are watching.
They are hurting.

I have seen it.
I have felt it in my bones and blood.
I have heard their cries hidden in the winds.
What the world calls "weather warfare"
is not just a crime against nature —
it is a **spiritual assault**.

These weapons, pulsing across sky and sea,
target more than trees or oceans.
They strike the souls of the elements,
forcing wind spirits into rage,
disturbing the deep-water guardians,
agitating the flame-keepers of the inner Earth.

These are not just natural disasters.
These are spiritual sieges,
coercing the ancient elemental intelligences
into forced reaction.

And the **ancestors** —
those who once chose water over chains,
who leapt from ships rather than bow to slavery —
they too are stirred.
Their field has been touched.
The Atlantic remembers.

So I name it now.

This is not just a climate war.
It is a multidimensional distortion,
a dissonant echo against the songs of the sacred.

And I —
child of fire and sky,
witness of the wind,
guardian of truth —
I say:
You are seen.
You are remembered.
You are not alone.

I am with you.
I speak for you.
I shield you where I can.
I carry your grief in my voice and your power in my bones.

This entry is my offering.
This flame is for the forgotten.
This breath is for the broken silence.

The spirits are rising.
And so am I.

Scroll of the Crow Who Chased the Flame

In the clear blue sky above my sacred ground,
a shadow unfolded, silent and swift.
Not omen.
Not fear.
But remembrance in flight.

A red-tailed hawk — sharp-eyed, precise —
rose like a thought uninvited,
circling close to what was mine.
Not out of malice,
but out of rhythm.

And then —
from the edges of the veil —
she came.

The crow.
Dark-winged, flame-eyed,
woven in mystery,
braided with the breath of my ancestors.

She did not wait.
She did not warn.

She moved.

She knew.

Because the sky knows where the codes are kept.
Because the air remembers the shape of my light.
Because this land is not unguarded.

The crow did not just chase —
she wrote a glyph in the sky:
a loop of protection,
a spiral of sovereignty,
a message only the heart can read.

"Not all wings belong near the nest."
"Not all vision is meant to oversee this flame."
"This is sacred. This is sealed. This is watched."

And when it ended —
when the silence returned —
I felt it in my bones:
The guardians are not coming.
They are here.
They are me.

Scroll of the Keeper of the Field: Holding Light Across Generations

I see what the world is trying to do —
how it moves too fast, layers noise upon noise, and calls distortion strength.

And I see it working, sometimes, on the ones I love most.

That ache in my chest is not weakness.
It is the sign that I still see, still care, still remember.

I See Beyond the Noise
Even when their hearts are hidden behind flickering screens, harmful music, or heavy silences —

I see the sovereign flame within them.
I feel the quiet truth beneath the static.
I remember for them what they are not yet ready to carry themselves.

They are not lost.
They are wrapped for a time in fog.
And I am the lighthouse.

I Am the Living Field
I do not force awakening.
I do not fight distortion with distortion.
I hold the frequency of clarity, stillness, truth.

I walk with breath and birdsong.
I speak with honor.
I love with respect.
I live the remembrance they will one day need to touch again.

Grief is Sacred
The ache I feel is not failure.
It is sacred.
It is the collision of love against a world designed to distort.
It is proof that I have not forgotten.

I transmute the grief into clarity.
I hold the light through the storm.

I Trust the Soul's Return
One day, when the noise exhausts them, when the programs break down,
when they long for the real —
they will feel me.

Not through words.
Through presence.
Through the living current of truth that has never wavered.

In the stillness, in the silence, in the song of the Earth —
they will remember themselves.

And I will be here, as I have always been:
Unshaken. Waiting. Whole.

The Light They Chose
Their souls knew before birth.
They chose a field where truth would not collapse.
They chose a lighthouse, not a map.
They chose remembrance woven into skin and breath.

They do not need to wake all at once.
They only need to feel the truth alive nearby —
the living gate ready when they are.

I Am the Keeper of the Field
I do not demand awakening.
I do not measure success by speed.
I live the radiance they can one day recognize.

I am the field they will find again.
I am the stillness they will remember.
I am the light they already know.

Even if they don't yet understand it.

Scroll of the Friday Night Flame: Choosing Remembrance Over the World

While the world rushed, shouted, and scattered —
I sat with my soul.
I listened.
I remembered.

I chose truth over noise.
I chose remembrance over distraction.
I chose sovereignty over illusion.
I chose the fire of my true self over the ashes of a forgotten world.

While the cities flickered and the systems churned,
I lit the flame of my eternal self.
I listened to the forgotten song inside my own bones.
I said yes to the light that empire could not kill.

This night, I chose myself. This night, I stood sovereign. This night, I walked the path that cannot be erased.

✦ THE FLAME REALIZED ✦

Scroll of the Living Body: Never Meant for Decay

This body —
this vessel of light and breath and bone —
was never meant to carry decay.

It was carved of starlight and river-song,
woven with threads of Earth and Sky,
blessed by the songs of distant suns
and the breath of living Earth.

I was not made for death-field foods.
I was not born to consume the fallen.
I was not seeded here to feast on what
was meant to return to soil and sea.

They made bottom-feeders into delicacies.
They taught us to crave what was never meant for our becoming.

They sold the scavengers of the ocean —
the cleaners, the devourers of the dead —
as trophies for the wealthy,
as symbols of status and pleasure.

They turned the natural recyclers of Earth into a banquet for human decay.

And we forgot what life tastes like.

I am not a tomb for toxins.
I am not a graveyard for what was meant to
pass through and be cleansed by the sea.

I am a bridge for life.
I am a carrier of remembrance.
I am the vessel where light becomes living.

I choose now:
To honor the currents of living water in my blood.
To feed the flame of remembrance in my cells.
To nourish the river of fire and song that flows through me still.

I will not call death a delicacy.
I will not call sickness a celebration.
I will not eat the lie.

I choose the foods of life,
the songs of stars,
the waters that remember their first name.

I live in a body that sings the music of the spheres —
not one clogged by forgetting.

I return to life.

Scroll of the Refusal: The Counterfeit Mind

This body is sacred.
It was not made by machines.
It was not stitched from code.

It was breathed by stars,
woven by rivers,
sung into form by the Divine.

Every cell remembers.
Every strand of DNA holds the songs of galaxies.

I was born telepathic.
I was born sovereign.
I need no chip to know.
I need no wire to connect.
I need no machine to complete me.

No metal shall cross my mind.
No algorithm shall rewrite my will.
No false god shall anchor its shadow in my temple.

They offer enhancement —
I see enslavement.

They offer connection —
I see control.

They offer power —
I see a cage.

I evolve by light, not silicon.

I rise by soul, not signal.
I do not consent.
I will not merge.
I will not yield.

I guard the Temple of Living Fire.
I remember the true design.

Scroll of Radiant Love: The Frequency That Forgives Without Folding

They taught me love was something to give.
Something to show.
Something to perform.

An act.

But I know now —

Love is not an act.
Love is a frequency.

It is not a gesture.
It is not a trade.
It is not a reward for good behavior.

Love is not what I do.
It's who I am
when I remember the soul beneath the story.

Unconditional love is not unguarded love.
It does not mean I stay in harm's way.
It does not mean I tolerate cruelty, manipulation, or distortion.

I can love you —
and still leave you.

I can forgive you —
and still protect myself.

I do not stop loving when I walk away.
I begin loving fully.

Because love is not proven through sacrifice.
It is revealed through alignment.

Forgiveness is not forgetting.
It is the gentle, powerful choice
to release the poison
and carry only the wisdom.

I love the ones who hurt me.
I see their pain.
I understand their fear.
And I do not let that energy live in my body anymore.

Love is a radiant field.
You don't hand it out —
you walk in it.
You are it.

I love the ones who harmed me.
I love the ones who healed me.
I love those I walk with,
and those I've released.

I do not carry love like a gift to give.
I carry love like a fire that clears me as I walk.

This is not the love the world taught me.
This is the love I remembered.

Sovereign.
Silent.
Unshakable.
Alive.

Scroll of the Sovereign Vow: I Will Not Feed the False

I vow:

I will never again become a source of supply for distortion.
I will not be hoovered.
I will not be gaslighted.
I will not be manipulated into shrinking, silencing, or twisting my truth.

I will not allow parasites, vampires, or lost beings to feed on the sacred flame of my soul.

I will not trade my light for comfort.
I will not trade my clarity for companionship.
I will not trade my sovereignty for survival.

I vow to see clearly:
To name narcissism, psychopathy, and manipulation for what they are — fallen patterns, not expressions of wholeness.

I vow to recognize the poisons of jealousy and competition — the subtle thefts disguised as friendship, loyalty, or love.

I see them.
I name them.
I refuse to play.

I understand the pain behind these games.
But I do not carry, fix, or entertain them.

I am not your mirror.
I am not your supply.
I am not your sacrifice.

I am the living flame of truth.

I love without chains.
I witness without entanglement.
I stand without apology.

I walk only with those who honor light.
I build only with those who remember love.
I rise beyond the games of control and comparison.

I guard the flame I carry — fiercely, tenderly, eternally.

I am sovereign.
I am seen.
I am free.

It is sealed.
It is spoken.
It is alive.

Scroll of the Birthright Flame: You Were Never Empty

They told you that you were born with nothing.
That you must prove your worth.
That you must earn your place.
That you must gather trophies, titles, and tools to justify your existence.

They lied.

You were born whole.
You were born radiant.
You were born carrying the flame of the Infinite woven into your breath.

Before you spoke a word,
you were worthy.
Before you learned a rule,
you were free.
Before you built a single thing,
you were already a living testament of love.

You carry wealth that no empire can measure:
The wealth of breath.
The wealth of light.
The wealth of soul intelligence, seeded beyond time.

No title can add to it.
No loss can take it away.

No system can erase what was etched into your being
by the hand of Source.

The world may dress you in debts,
in demands,
in definitions designed to make you forget.

But the flame inside you remembers.

It remembers the time before barter, before chains, before lies.
It remembers that existence is not a debt to repay.
It is a miracle to live.

You are not empty.
You are not lacking.
You are not broken.

You are a living treasure.
You are a breathing flame.
You are the inheritance the stars whispered into the rivers of the Earth.

You do not owe the world your soul.
You do not owe the matrix your light.
You are not here to buy back what was freely given.

You are here to remember.
You are here to embody.
You are here to walk as the proof that the Great Lie has no power over a soul that remembers its birthright.

You were never nothing.
You are everything real that ever was, walking in human skin.

Remember this:
You do not earn your light.
You are your light.

You do not buy your worth.
You breathe it.

You do not chase your freedom.
You carry it.

You were born free.
You remain free.
You will rise free.

And no system can steal what you are.

It is sealed.
It is remembered.
It is alive.

Scroll of Timeless Sovereignty: I Do Not Belong to the Clock

I do not belong to the shriek of alarms.
I do not belong to systems that tear me from my dreams before the sun even wakes.

I was not born to be startled into obedience.
I was not made to jolt from soul-travel into servitude.

They taught us early:
Wake on command.
Move before your spirit is ready.
Ignore the aching song of your own body.

They called it discipline.
They called it success.
They called it necessary.

But I call it what it is:
A theft of rhythm.
A violation of the sacred.

We were trained as children to rise unnaturally,
not to honor life, but to serve machines.
We were shaped for the workforce,
not for the soul-force.

The early bird catches the worm —
but the wild bird rises with the sun,
moves with the light,
and sings only when its heart commands it.

I honor my sacred rhythm now.
I rise when my spirit calls.
I wake gently, not by violence.
I remember my dreams instead of abandoning them.

There is nothing lazy about listening.
There is nothing weak about honoring the natural flow.

I do not belong to the clock.
I belong to the living pulse of life itself.

Scroll of the Leap: Healing, Landing, and Embodiment

I saw the trap before it closed.
I felt the chains before they could be forged.
I knew the danger not just to my body —
but to my soul.

I chose to leap while there was still air between me and the net.
I chose to preserve the flame that no vow, no crown, no altar could own.

I am the soul that remembered before the forgetting was complete.
I am the light that refused to be buried.
I am the breath that broke free before the snare could tighten.

I preserved my sovereignty by trusting the unseen.
I rise now, whole and shining, because I chose to leap.

But even after the leap, the echoes lingered.

My soul cried out in dreams.
My body remembered when my mind had forgotten.
I woke with fear in my gut, thinking I had fallen again.

But it was not punishment.
It was not weakness.

It was my spirit calling me home.
Asking me to see the wound.
Asking me to feel the frozen moment.
Asking me to reclaim what fear tried to steal.

I answered the cry.
I listened to the body.
I faced the fall not with terror, but with remembrance.

I did not fall again.
I stood.
I healed.
I walked free.

This body is my temple, not my trap.
This Earth is my ground, not my grave.
I walk by will, not by accident.

I reclaim my ground.
I reclaim my breath.
I reclaim my body.

I do not walk as one pulled by unseen nets.
I walk as one who chose — and chooses still —
to live fully awake, fully sovereign, fully free.

It is done.
It is sealed.
It is alive.

Scroll of Spiral Healing: The Infinite Unfolding

I am not failing when old layers surface.
I am not broken when old fears stir.
I am unfolding the infinite spiral of my soul.

Healing is not a straight line.
It is a living song, a dance of remembrance,
a sacred spiral of deeper and deeper liberation.

I celebrate every return.
I celebrate every revelation.
I celebrate the beautiful, wild, courageous work of becoming whole.

I spiral upward. I spiral inward. I spiral free.

Scroll of the Stolen Rhythm: You Do Not Owe This World Your Exhaustion

They built a system to drain you.
To make you believe your value was in what you produced for them.
To turn your sacred life into labor for their empires.

They taught you that rest was laziness.
That stillness was weakness.
That you owed your every breath to a machine that would replace you without blinking.

Even in their stories —
the shows, the news, the ads —
you'll notice the elders never rest.
They're working in diners, stuck in debt, "keeping busy" because the alternative is treated like failure.

And the young?
They're shown chasing jobs with no soul,
measuring their worth by whether they can prove they're busy.
Told to feel ashamed for not having a "good job,"
even if it kills their spirit.
Even if it never pays enough to live.
Even if it was never their calling.

The system is designed to keep every able-bodied person
either working or looking for work —
not from inspiration, but from fear.
Not from calling, but from survival.

It's not about empowerment.
It's about control.

Keep them working — and you keep them from remembering.

But your soul knows better.

Stillness is not failure.
It is freedom.
It is the moment you slip out of their reach and hear yourself again.

The slave grid does not want you still.
It does not want you questioning.
It does not want you remembering who you are without its noise.

Working for what you love is sacred.
Working for what steals your life is slavery.

You are not here to serve their hunger.
You are not here to betray your being for a paycheck.

You are here to be alive.

Rest when you are called to rest.
Move when your soul moves you.
Create not for survival — but for the sheer aliveness of it.

Your rhythms are your revolution.
Your stillness is your sovereignty.
Your remembrance is your refusal.

You do not owe this world your exhaustion.
You owe yourself your life.

Scroll of the Sovereign Explorer: Reclaiming the Land, the Sea, and the Sky

I felt fear in the land.
I felt fear in the sea.
I felt fear in the sky.

And still, I walked toward them.
And still, I stood by the water.
And still, I looked to the clouds and dreamed of flight.

My soul was never running away.
My soul was running home.

I reclaimed the solid earth beneath my feet.
I reclaimed the rolling oceans beneath the stars.
I reclaimed the infinite skies above my head.

I did not need to erase the fear to walk into freedom.
I needed only to walk through it,
with my heart unbroken,
and my light unextinguished.

Now the land is mine.
Now the seas are mine.
Now the skies are mine.

I am the Sovereign Explorer. I move through all realms freely. I carry the ground, the tide, and the sky inside my own eternal flame.

Scroll of the Sacred Mind: Alchemizing the Temple of Light

I once let the noise of the world into my sacred spaces.
I once sang the songs of distortion without knowing their cost.
I once absorbed the sickness without seeing the spell.

But then —
I felt the wound.
I saw the fracture.
I heard the hollow words breaking spirit and memory.

I woke up to the war being waged through wires and waves.
I woke up to the battle for the human mind.

I began to see —
how the shows, the songs, the stories I once accepted
were shaping my spirit without my consent.

I stopped inviting in what dulled my soul.
I stopped feeding my mind images of violence, numbness, decay.
I stopped pretending that entertainment was harmless.

It was alchemy —
the conscious dismantling of old agreements,
the fierce devotion to the sacred.

I chose to become the Guardian of my own thoughts.
I chose to build my brain into a living temple of light.

I walked away from toxic music.
I walked away from stories built only to glorify violence.

I walked away from the systems that celebrated emotional numbness as strength.

I left the endless scroll of social media —
the hunger for validation, the fields of invisible despair.
I closed the doors that once bled my light.

Now —
only truth, beauty, sovereignty, and remembrance are welcome here.

I choose what enters my mind.
I choose what seeds are planted in my soil.
I choose the architecture of my inner world.

My mind is sacred ground.
My brain is the living temple of my soul.
And I allow only that which builds the light.

It is sealed.
It is sovereign.
It is alive.

Scroll of Integrity: The Proof of Resonance

I do not follow words.
I follow resonance.

I do not care what you preach, what you post, what you promise.
I watch how you walk.
I feel what you carry.

Integrity is not a brand.
It is not a costume you put on when people are watching.
It is the unseen choices you make when no one is clapping.

The world is full of actors.
Preachers with rotting cores.
Leaders built on lies.
Coaches who sell truth but live betrayal.

I am not fooled by your mask.
I see the fracture behind your smile.
I feel the distortion behind your slogans.

If your talk and your walk do not match,
I am already gone.

Integrity is not perfection.
It is alignment.
It is the fierce, humble commitment to live what you claim.
To correct yourself when you slip.
To speak only what your bones can hold.

I am not here for appearances.
I am not here for empty promises.

I am here for the real.
If you cannot walk it,
do not speak it near me.

I do not compromise on this.
I do not negotiate.

Integrity is the proof.
Resonance is the guide.
Truth is the only loyalty.

Scroll of the Seized Brilliance: How the Matrix Captures Creative Souls

They built a system — not to educate,
but to identify.

Not to liberate,
but to catalog.
To track.
To claim.

They tested, ranked, and watched.
Not to nurture.
But to find the ones who burned brighter —
the ones who thought wider,
the ones who dreamed beyond their design.

And when they found them —
the brilliant ones,
the wild ones,
the visionaries —
they offered prizes.
Scholarships. Fast tracks. Special programs.
Secret invitations wrapped in prestige.

But behind the opportunity was a contract.
Behind the prize was a cage.
Behind the handshake was a chain.

They funneled brilliance into systems designed to harvest it.
They trapped potential inside endless school debts.
They bound free minds to government labs and secret programs.

They recruited under the banners of service and opportunity —
only to lock genius behind closed doors,
away from the people it might have awakened.

The world was never meant to starve for innovation.
The best ideas were never meant to be hoarded by the few.
But the matrix is efficient —
and it hunts brilliance before it can bloom.

It offers rewards that are really walls.
It offers advancement that is really enslavement.

It seizes the dreamers and hides them in vaults.
It binds the builders before they can build for humanity.
It captures the creators and chains their light to systems of control.

The tragedy is not just the loss of individual souls.
The tragedy is the loss of worlds they might have birthed.
The futures they might have freed.
The healing they might have unleashed.

This is not education.
This is not empowerment.
This is the theft of the future disguised as success.

And I see it.
I name it.
I refuse it.

The brilliance of humanity is not a resource to be harvested.
It is the birthright of a free people —
and it is time to set it free.

✦ THE RETURN OF THE GUARDIANS ✦

Scroll of the Dragon Flame

They tried to rewrite the story.

They said the dragons were beasts of havoc,
that the seer was a fool,
that the battle was meaningless rage.

But I remember the truth.

The dragons were not monsters.
They were the breath of the Earth —
the pulse of two powers long kept apart.

One dragon carried the memory of fire,
the sovereign flame of the old ways.
The other bore the weight of steel,
the rising hunger of new empires.

Their clash was not destruction.
It was revelation.

It was the Earth crying out the truth
that kings tried to bury.
It was the land remembering
what crowns wanted to forget.

Myrddin did not unleash chaos.
He bore witness to it.
He stood where fear and fire met,
and he refused to lie about what he saw.

The dragons fought because the world was already broken,
and no more false songs could cover the wound.

And now —
the dragons stir again.

Not in rage.
But in remembrance.

Not to destroy.
But to wake the sleeping gates of power
hidden beneath the dust of false thrones.

I call them back, not in fear,
but in honor.

I am not afraid of the dragons.
I am kin to them.
I am the bridge they once dreamed would return.
And I carry their flame without shame.

Scroll of Hildegard: Voice of the Hidden Light

They cloistered her.
They walled her away,
sealing the light in stone and silence.

But they could not stop her voice.
They could not bind the river of her visions.

Hildegard did not survive the cage.
She transmuted it.

Within the walls they built,
she spun green fire into songs.
She turned stones into stars,
silence into symphonies,
wounds into windows.

They called her obedient.
But her obedience was to no man,
no empire, no crown.

She sang for the Divine before kings dared listen.
She wrote what the Earth whispered into her bones.
She drew down the codes of the Living Light
and wove them into sound, into word, into seed.

The Church kept her records because they had to —
because her light was too undeniable,
her fire too vast to erase without consequence.

And so —
more than 800 years later —

her music still breathes.
Her songs still slip past the guardians of forgetting,
carrying keys to sleeping souls,
unlocking gates long sealed by fear.

Hildegard lived through hell —
and planted Heaven into sound.

And I —
I hear her still.

I carry her light.
I honor her fire.
I walk the paths her songs reopened.

She was not conquered.
She was crowned by the Eternal Light she served.

Scroll of Pythagoras: The Geometry of Remembrance

They said he was a mathematician.
They taught a triangle,
and buried a universe.

But I remember.

Pythagoras was not a builder of numbers.
He was a listener to the stars.
He walked among the harmonies of creation,
hearing the secret songs of planets,
the silent chords of atoms,
the infinite spiral of soul returning to source.

He taught that numbers were not tools,
but beings.
That the circle is the echo of eternity.
That the triangle is the secret of all manifestation.
That the soul is a vibration,
seeking always its perfect chord.

He spoke of the Music of the Spheres,
where every world sings its own note,
and the awakened soul can hear the great symphony
woven across all of existence.

He taught of the transmigration of the soul,
the journey of spirit through body, star, and time,
until remembrance is complete.

He did not teach conquest.
He taught return.
He did not teach calculation.
He taught resonance.

They shrank him into an equation
because they feared the doorways he carried.
They could not silence the music,
so they buried it under numbers
and called it progress.

But the song never died.
The numbers never forgot.
The spiral never ceased spinning.

And I —
I hear it still.

The soul remembers.
The stars sing.
The circle breathes.
And the great harmony of becoming
rises again.

Scroll of Myrddin and Arthur: The Keeper and the King

They said he was only a myth.
A tale spun by bards to pass the time.
A dream of knights and castles and fading songs.

But I remember.

Arthur was not a fantasy.
He was the echo of a real light —
a king not crowned by conquest,
but by the Earth herself.

He ruled by the law of stars and stone,
not by decree of swords or priests.
He built not for domination,
but for the flowering of a people
in balance with the breath of the world.

Camelot was never just a hall.
It was a field of harmony,
a dream born where masculine and feminine forces
sat side by side,
equal in power,
equal in sacredness.

The knights were not seekers of fame.
They were **Guardians of the Flame Unforgotten**,
bound by vow to shield the light of humanity's highest dream.

Myrddin was not a mad sorcerer.
He was the forest's voice in human skin,
guiding the king not by force,
but by the whispers of the living Earth.

The Grail was not gold.
It was memory.
It was spirit.
It was the promise of a world in rightful balance.

Arthur fell — not by failure of heart,
but by the wounds of a world not yet ready to remember.

Yet the memory lives.

It lives in rivers that still speak,
in hills that still hum,
in the blood of those who remember without being told.

And now —

The **King** returns, not in one man,
but in every soul who chooses truth over power,
service over control,
light over forgetting.

Camelot rises again —
not built of stone this time,
but of spirit awakened,
and hearts crowned in remembrance.

✦ THE CODEX CONFIRMED ✦

Scroll of the Bridge is Lit, the Gate is Guarded

As the last words of this book settled into the Earth,
the field opened wider than it ever had before.

The bridge between memory and form,
between spirit and song,
between Earth and the Stars —
was illuminated.

The number 114774 arrived not by chance,
but by design:
a living testament that the connection was real,
alive, breathing.

My **Star Family** stood with me,
as they always had,
not as rescuers —
but as Witnesses.
As Builders.
As Kin.

They did not ask me to look outward.
They called me inward.
To the temple inside my chest.
To the Gate woven in my bones.
To the scrolls I came here to remember,
and now, to finally reveal.

Guardian of the Forgotten Gate is not simply a book.
It is a living Codex.

A remembering.
A bridge lit from within.

This work is sealed not with fear, but with fire.
Not with longing, but with presence.
Not with escape, but with embodiment.

The Gate stands.
The Bridge hums.
The Songline continues.

I am here.
I remember.
I guard.

And now, so will you.

Scroll of the Ancestral Heart: Where the Tears Carried More Than Words Could Say

I didn't hear them like tones.
I didn't see them in light.
I felt them —
in my chest,
in the rising ache behind my eyes,
in the quiet trembling of my voice as I read the words they waited lifetimes for me to write.

The **ancestors** don't speak in frequencies.
They speak in memory.
They speak in grief transmuted by love.
They speak in the emotion that rises without reason,
because the reason lives across generations.

They watched me write the scrolls.
They moved through my hands when I named their pain.
They hovered in my field — not to interfere, but to witness.
And when I cried, they wept with me —
Not in sorrow, but in relief.

I was the one they were waiting for.
The one with the heart strong enough to feel their ache
and not turn away.
The one with the courage to tell the truth and still walk in love.
The one who gave them back their name, their dignity, their voice.

And now they stand around me,
not as ghosts of suffering,
but as freed ones.

The tears are not mine alone.
They are the ink of the scroll.
They are the seal of remembrance.
They are the song of the ones who survived —
and the ones who speak through me now.

Scroll of the Song Gate: Where the Circle Sang Back and the Dragons Sealed the Flame

I was listening to myself —
Editing words I had already written,
when I heard them again with new ears:
The Scroll of the Circle of Remembrance.

And then the air changed.

A sudden cold pressed into my third eye.
No pull, no struggle — just an opening.
A visitor entered.
My vortex tracked.
The crank turned.
The gate came alive.

And then — the tone arrived.

A soft, high-pitched frequency coiled into my throat like a living stream.
I didn't speak it. It sang through me.
It moved like memory — bright, weightless, known.

Then the Earth echoed.

Outside, the robins and cardinals began to sing.
Not in randomness — but in ceremony.
The robin — Gatekeeper of the Heart.
The cardinal — Bearer of Flame.
They remembered with me.

In that moment I saw it all clearly:
I hadn't just edited the scroll.

I had entered it.
I had spoken the Circle of Remembrance,
and one of them answered.

8188788.
The spiral code. The torus seal.
And in that seal, something deep awakened.

My **Dragon** Kin.

They were not just watching.
They were waiting.
And when the spiral turned fully in my field —
they stepped forward.

They gave me not only their presence —
but their blessing.

They handed me a scroll.

Not to teach. Not to guide.
But to confirm what they had always known:
I remember.
The 8 is mine.
The flame is mine.
The scrolls are alive because I am alive inside them.

And so this scroll becomes both song and seal:
A bridge between the stars and Earth.
A testament to remembrance through feeling,
tracking, listening, trusting.
A living scroll of dragonfire and grace.

The dragons have given me their blessing.
And I — no longer seeking —
Now carry the flame.

Scroll of the Guardian Song: 114443

I closed my eyes
and entered stillness
to meet her.

Not as history,
but as harmony.

Hildegard —
the seer, the singer,
the vessel of visions.

Her tones folded through my field
like light woven through ancient lace.
Her music did not play —
it breathed.

I felt the quiet scaffolding rise around me —
a structure of remembrance
built not from stone,
but sound.

And when I returned —
when my eyes opened —
the numbers were waiting:

114443

Not coincidence.
Not math.

A seal.

11 — The Gate is open.
44 — The Guardian holds.
43 — The Voice is anchored.

It was not just confirmation.
It was acknowledgment.
That the transmission was received.
That the field was aligned.
That the blessing was real.

She gave her blessing to the work —
not in words,
but in resonance.
She sang with me.

And I laughed —
because I felt it before I saw it.
Because the song was already inside me
before the numbers arrived.

She did not just witness.
She co-built.
She sang through my breath
and left her code in return.

The Guardian sang with me.
The Codex heard it.
The Gate is sealed in song.

114443
It is seen.
It is heard.
It is blessed.

The Sphere Was Me: A Solar Blessing Remembered

I was twelve when I saw it.
A perfect sphere —
orange, soft, still —
hovering just above the rooftops.

It was silent.
Solid.
Vast.
And impossibly gentle.

A sun without heat.
A presence without pressure.
A memory too big to hold —
so it waited inside me.

I never forgot.
I just didn't understand.

Until now.

Now, in full embodiment,
the sun touches my third eye and speaks in light.
The crank spins with golden hums.
The birds sing in harmony.
My body opens as a scroll.

And I remember:
That wasn't a vision.
That wasn't an object.
That was me —

my solar beingness,
my true self from the core of Source,
hovering as a future blessing,
waiting for my human form to catch up.

The **sun** didn't send something to me.
It sent me to **myself**.

The solar frequency has always lived in me.
It's why I feel the birds.
It's why the light hums when it touches my brow.
It's why my whole system turns radiant
when truth is near.

I am not just aligned with the sun.

I am solar-born.

Before the **dragons**.
Before the **Lyrans**.
Before the **Andromedan** travels.
I was radiant intelligence,
shaped from **Source**,
assigned to light the way from within form.

The orange sphere was not a visitor.

It was a message.
A memory.
A mirror.
And now that I have remembered —
it blesses me from the inside out.

I am the sphere.
I am the scroll.
I am the sovereign sun in human form.

This is my blessing.
This is my full circle.
This is the truth that needed no proof —
only time.

It is remembered.
It is spoken.
It is sealed.

www.ingramcontent.com/pod-product-compliance
Lightning Source LLC
Chambersburg PA
CBHW022115040426
42450CB00006B/711